WHERE'S TRUMP?

Illustrated by
Anastasia Catris

This edition first published in Great Britain in 2016
by Orion
an imprint of the Orion Publishing Group Ltd
Carmelite House, 50 Victoria Embankment
London EC4Y 0DZ
An Hachette UK Company

3 5 7 9 10 8 6 4 2

A CIP catalogue record for this book
is available from the British Library.

Hardback ISBN: 978 1 4091 6773 0

Printed in Italy

Every effort has been made to fulfil requirements
with regard to reproducing copyright material.
The author and publisher will be glad to rectify
any omissions at the earliest opportunity.

This book is a parody and has not been prepared,
endorsed or sponsored by Donald Trump.

www.orionbooks.co.uk

INTRODUCTION

Welcome to the world of Trump, where money speaks louder than words (but loud words are also good) and offensive diatribe is the order of the day. Sometimes it feels like Trump is everywhere; on our TVs, making headlines, and just when you thought you were safe, he's an internet meme! Love, loathe or laugh at, Donald Trump is unavoidable.

Never one to normally get lost in a crowd, Donald is now hidden amongst the masses in his gold-plated race to the White House. Can you track him down?

Is Donald J about to make a smackdown at a wrestling match? Is that Trump carving his face into Mount Rushmore? Oh boy, here comes a helluva vehicle – is he aboard the Trump Train? Only the meanest, keenest searchers will be able to spot The Donald alongside the good ol' working people of the US of A.

Plus, for those who want more (and remember, you can never be too greedy), there are tons of extras to search out. Go through the 'What to Find on Each Page' section that follows and tick off all you can. Then do a big Trumpette twirl and give yourself a high five if you can relate the object to one of Trump's finest moments.

Remember – brash, cash and white trash are key when it comes to finding Trump! Follow the money and get hunting!

Ps. This is a Trumpathon, not a sprint. So pace yourself.

WHAT TO FIND ON EACH PAGE

On every page

- [ ] Donald Trump (always with wild hair and wearing a red tie)
- [ ] Sarah 'hockey mom' Palin
- [ ] Trump hairpiece

- [ ] Obama's birth certificate
- [ ] Diet coke
- [ ] Red cap
- [ ] Handgun

1. Trump Force One

- [ ] Michael Jackson
- [ ] American eagle
- [ ] Pile of money
- [ ] Leopard print sleeping mask
- [ ] Golden sink
- [ ] Smell of success aftershave

- [ ] Trump jacket
- [ ] Yards of silks
- [ ] *Air Force One* DVD
- [ ] Gold lifejacket
- [ ] American Psycho

2. You're Fired

- [ ] Trump jacket
- [ ] Smell of success aftershave
- [ ] Yellow taxi cab
- [ ] Donald Trump's CV
- [ ] Flirting group of girls
- [ ] The Governator
- [ ] American Psycho
- [ ] Trump doll
- [ ] Lord Alan Sugar in a classic pinstripe suit
- [ ] Pile of money

3. Tea Time at Capitol Hill

- [ ] American Psycho
- [ ] Mad Hatter and Alice at a tea party
- [ ] Gadsden Flag
- [ ] Bible basher in a tricorne hat
- [ ] Macaulay Culkin
- [ ] Patriotic teapot
- [ ] Bison logo
- [ ] Obama Bin Lyin' banner
- [ ] Uncle Sam
- [ ] Hillary Clinton behind bars
- [ ] Trump jacket

4. A**hole in One

- [ ] Pile of money
- [ ] Man trying to hold down his kilt
- [ ] American flag
- [ ] Trump Towers sandcastle
- [ ] Diamante golf clubs
- [ ] William Wallace
- [ ] Nicola Sturgeon
- [ ] A conveniently placed balloon
- [ ] Pimped up golf buggy

5. The Great Wall of Trump

- [ ] Smell of success aftershave
- [ ] Man in a white wall onesie
- [ ] Man dressed as a cactus
- [ ] Trump piñata
- [ ] Pile of money
- [ ] A night watchman
- [ ] Mariachi band
- [ ] A topless worker
- [ ] A discarded sombrero

6. Mount Trumpmore

- [ ] Bigfoot
- [ ] Fools mining for gold
- [ ] Graffiti artist
- [ ] Presidential gold tooth
- [ ] Boy stuck in Trump's hair
- [ ] American bald eagle nest
- [ ] Solo selfie-taker
- [ ] Some confused hikers
- [ ] Smell of success aftershave

7. Trump Towers

- [ ] White fluffy cat
- [ ] Gold spray paint
- [ ] American Psycho
- [ ] Pretzel
- [ ] Trump coat
- [ ] Trump library
- [ ] Ice cream
- [ ] Smell of success aftershave
- [ ] Gold toilet roll
- [ ] Pile of money
- [ ] I heart NY shirt
- [ ] Throne
- [ ] Gold bricks
- [ ] 3 x BigBucks coffee cups

8. Trump Train

- [ ] American eagle
- [ ] Cherry coke
- [ ] Hamburgers and peanuts lunchbox
- [ ] 3 'Trumpette' Trump girls
- [ ] Miss Galaxy
- [ ] 2 LGBT shirts
- [ ] Champagne

9. White House

- [ ] Bouncer to the Trump club
- [ ] Toga party
- [ ] Trump gold statue
- [ ] Hillary Clinton
- [ ] Flying pig
- [ ] Pile of money
- [ ] Bars of gold
- [ ] High heeled volleyball player
- [ ] Playboy bunnies

10. Ring Stinger

- [ ] Tan-in-a-can
- [ ] Hulk Hogan
- [ ] God of War muscle juice
- [ ] Can of shaving foam
- [ ] Pile of money
- [ ] Vince McMahon getting his head shaved
- [ ] Confederate flag

Trump Force One

The Trump has landed. Turbulence follows The Donald around like a lingering smell, but who cares if the ride was bumpy, now he's back on solid ground. It's time to roll out the red carpet, get your touchdown party banners out and start finding Trump!

You're Fired

As a famous Swedish band once sang, 'Money money money, must be funny, in a rich man's world'. But this is no laughing matter. People are busy climbing the greasy pole to win a job but Trump has gone AWOL. He needs to be found, otherwise 'you're fired!'.

Tea Time at Capitol Hill

The Donald enjoys a little tea party now and again. But you haven't got time to pour yourself a cuppa, there's a dangerously powerful billionaire on the loose in this sea of red, white and blue! Careful not to be distracted by mad hatters, Marxist liars or Sarah Palin.

A**hole in One

Don't keep your head buried in the sand bunker. It's time to tee off and find Donald Trump amid the holes and balls of the golf course. Double bogey! Fore!

The Great Wall of Trump

Everybody needs good neighbours. And what better neighbour than Trump? He's the best wall-builder known to man! You just need to pay for the privilege (and maybe do the hard graft too). Once you've tracked him down, that is.

Mount Trumpmore

He always wanted to be a towering, stony-faced big head with a rock solid reputation – so that's why Trump is carving himself into Mount Rushmore. Plus, he's going bigger, better, bolder and golder than the founding fathers. Go Trump!

Trump Towers

Nothing oozes more class than riding a golden escalator to work. If it's not shiny, then Trump doesn't want to know, capish? Can you find Donald in his shrine to capitalism?

Trump Train

Honk honk! All aboard the Trump train! If you don't like what he has to say, then get outta the way. It's full steam ahead for railroading the voters now. So get your first class ticket and hop on while you search for Donald J. Trump.

White House

The circus has come to town! Oh no, wait . . . it's just the White House with a trump makeover. Neon lights and show-stopping laydeez are the very emblems of democracy, right? Try to find Donald while he's taking a break from his diplomatic duties.

REMOVALS

Ring Stinger

It's the final showdown but who is going to take the smackdown? Trump loves a bit of one-to-one combat and wrestling is a surefire favourite. It's entertainment-based muscle-flexing. Perfect! Just find the Trumpster throwing his weight around before the ultimate hostile takeover.

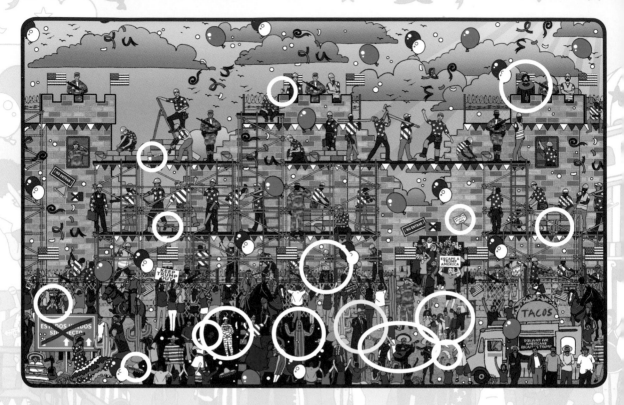
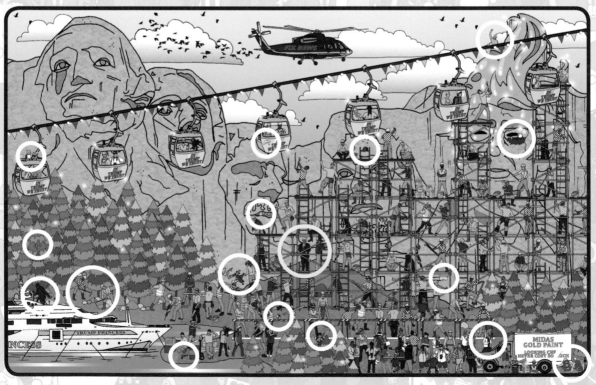

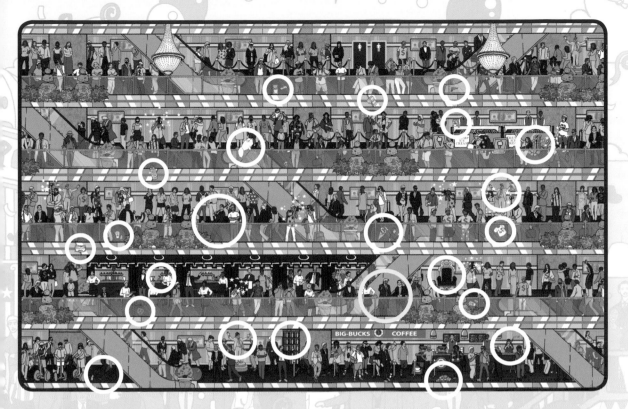